3 A.M
HEARTBREAK MATERIAL
BY MARISA CRANE

UNDERWATER MOUNTAINS PUBLISHING
LOS ANGELES, CALIFORNIA
A SECRET COMPANY.

For anyone who has ever lost sleep over love.

3 A.M. HEARTBREAK MATERIAL
MARISA CRANE

INTRODUCTION:
INTIMACY

I don't know a lot but this much I know to be true: if you want to know who someone is, you know, the true meat of someone, don't ask them what they do for work. That won't reveal much about their vessels, just the skin that protects them.

Instead, ask them what they think about at 3 A.M., what breaks their heart, whether they're a happy or sad drunk and why they think that is. Ask what their favorite book is, and smile as they ramble on about a character. Ask them if they ever dream that their teeth are falling out. If they answer "yes," give them a compliment, a genuine one. This means they're having self-image issues. Ask them to tell you about their childhood pet and watch their eyes light up in remembrance.

These things, I'm certain of it, will reveal someone far more intimately than the topic of work. We aren't what we do, but rather, what we feel, what cracks our bones, and how we deal with throbbing anguish. Asking someone what they "do" is just a more polite way of saying you don't give a fuck.

PART ONE:
YOU'D THINK MY LIVER BROKE MY HEART

wake up drunk and
examine my limbs,
all attached and
appear to be working.
I'm not dead so I
guess I'll go breathe
more stories into
the old typer.

it's morning and I can't
get enough of your warm,
coffee skin,
inviting me back to bed.
your steam rises, eloquently,
and begs for me to stay
a while,
and just like that,
I develop a terrible cough,
"so sorry, i'm sick,
I can't come into work today"

I quite enjoy cursing
and calling it poetry
but never again will I
fuck and refer to it
as love.

I don't deserve you. that
much I know to be true,
but as I stir your love into
my morning coffee, I notice
the virgin light leaking in
through the blinds,
and it reminds me that I have
yet another day to keep
trying my damnedest to.

if you think
losing a lover
is hard, then
try losing
a muse.

the silence
is deafening.

You'd think
my liver
broke my heart
the way
I abuse it
on a nightly basis.

once you start
smoking cigarettes
simply because dying
is just
a little bit easier
than doing
nothing at all,
then, and only then,
will you understand
the smoldering sadness
born in my mangled bones,
the very poisons intended to
distract me from myself

if you're going to
make me melt
night after night
in these sheets,
the least you could
do is leave a stack
of quarters on my
bedside table for
the laundry the
next morning.

I've had someone fuck me
without making me come
and I've has somebody
love me without ever
sacrificing a damn thing.

I can't for the life
of me figure out
which is worse.

All things
should be
made of the
bare threads
that line your
delicate
collarbone.

wine will do that to you.
make you think you're
in love at the
turn of the clocks
and delude you enough
to think that that matters.

it's politics, it's science
the way my demons join
your falsetto right on
through the night,
but don't expect my angels
to lie with your
celestial body
in the morning.

sunday mornings are for shower sex
sessions that set off the smoke detector
and make you late for work.
they're for leaving stray thongs
and empty bottles where they fell
and planning tattoo sleeves I'm never
going to get (literary themed).

tell me you can fathom the brooding atoms
within me, my lovely inferno and
cadaverous chamber
and I'll be sure to follow you anywhere,
for, you're better than dreams,
a shapeshifter of madness and worship.

I watch you whip up breakfast,
smothered in pancake batter and
intoxicating promise, you laugh
as you say that we made it this morning
like it was a goddamn revelation.

"how could you ever be
anything but mine?"

"I don't know, baby."

"the scariest moment of
my life will come the day
that you have an answer
to that."

If it's all the same
to you,
I prefer to watch
your silhouette as
you leave.
From where I'm sitting
it looks like
you're simply getting up
to get a glass of water
after sex.

these sloppy weekend mornings,
make-up smeared,
clothes strewn,
hungover from
drinking you in all night.
my stomach churns
as I roll over to find
that the dent in the mattress
is all that's left of you.
this whiskey tastes sour
when hair of the dog
looks more like
holding you.

If I end up like Hem,
blowing my brains into
my morning orange juice,
just know that I will
have wasted some
fine champagne, too.

on days like today
I'm inclined to hope
that this life is
merely a hangover
from a much more
prolific existence.

I think after
all this time,
I may be in love.

stranger things
have happened.

If I'm being honest
almost all of the memories I have of us
are imagined,
born into wrinkles of my mind
and ironing out the love we
never got to share.
I constantly dream of the words
we never said,
the ones in parentheses,
and of laughter I tell myself
we manufactured in the sun's rays-
cancelled smiles that never got
a chance to form.

I hoard syllables gone astray
and muffled vowels I extracted
from these sheets.
There are few things I know better
than the language of you and there's no
braille, no texture,
that reads exactly the same
as the smoothness of your skin,
the very grace I've always known
yet haven't felt.

free will is the reason
shakespeare wrote tragedies
and why everyone always ended up
dead,
the reason for sleeping pills
and alcohol, weed and codeine.
it's responsible for armies
waging war like children
arguing on the playground-
shooting marbles and beliefs
down the throats of fellow man.
it makes for a queasy sunday morning
reviewing the previous night's
debauchery
and playing dumb to the violence
screaming in your face.

above all else,
free will is witnessing the
salted sadness decorate my
hollow cheeks and still
choosing to leave,
anyway.

there have been 20 or so fatal
shootings in philly within
the past few days.
my mother called me up
to urge me to move,
and I don't blame her.
she doesn't want me to die,
no not just yet.

it's curious, then, that she
never demanded for me to
leave your side.

it's you.
it's always been you.
you came from the edges
of heaven,
the fringes of light and
all its rays.
the place where your halo
would sometimes slip off and
the devils would worship you.
if freckles are marks from
angel kisses,
then allow me to explore your
uncharted skin and kiss all
the spots those
careless angels missed.

I think I thought that if I fell
in love with the idea of love
hard enough,
then I could learn to be yours.
but life doesn't work that way
and as it turns out,
I wasn't your mess to clean up

we listened to alt-j all morning,
sipping irish coffees and
floating on whistling love.
it didn't take long for me to realize
that it was the enough
I'd always begged the universe
to give me

I urge you to love her fiercely,
mercilessly, and unapologetically.
play with the balls of fire in your palms
and burn off the life lines you formed
from an empty life before her.
go to the place where the flames
lick her wounds.
that's where you'll find her
constellations hiding,
they'll whisper tales of agony.
I beg you to listen.
and just promise me that the
next time she burns,
she burns for romantic ecstasies.

the way I see it,
you could rattle the
tectonic plates and
turn the world inside-out,
if you wanted.
and I believe in you
like I believe
I'm 17 again.

I woke up to find you
coloring my atmosphere.
at work at your easel,
a cigarette dangling
from your sultry lips,
your smile doused in
a whiskey high, I took
a hit of your sickness and
I tell you, it was
something fucking fierce,
something visceral and
squalor-induced. you
admitted to yourself to
my asylum with a goddamn
grin on your mug.

how exhausting it is
to think that human
beings invented time
and now we are all
slaves to the
ticking.

it was rather strange
to hear my love
describe me,
in detail
back to myself,
because it sounded
nothing like the
monster I'd always
contrived myself to be.

what if home was never a place
of comfort? what if its walls
contained years of abuse,
and emotions that eventually
turned to stone? I don't know
at what point everyone
went crazy but I
do know that the pills no longer
kept the demons at bay.

so, darling, ask me again if
you feel like home to me
then smile and kiss me
when I softly answer, "no"

you spoke to me in tongues as you
read Naked Lunch aloud from across
the heroin-white couch. It could have
been the whitest sand of beaches I'm
too poor to travel to.

                lathered on your brown skin,
                I loved the contrast but hated
                to compare

you were never the same as
the others, my muse,
my vigilante of the written word,
the banned book I risked hiding
under my mattress, anyway.

there's nothing worse than
waking up to find there's
no sky today.
stuck in this purgatory,
I'm wedged between
moving on
and you.

you once told me that
I was it for you,
that I was the end
to the blurry mess
you'd been spiraling in
for years on end.
but it's scary with your
eyes wide open,
tunnels connecting you to me,
and only now do I understand
that you didn't leave
because you wanted to,
but because you didn't like
what you saw.

PART TWO:
LAUGHING AT THE TRIVIALITY OF IT ALL

I was rainfall
in those days.

You were the floods
I caused.

And I could never
save us both.

leave it to you
and your addictive skin
to give "oral fixation"
a whole new meaning

I've been carelessly threaded
with broken buttons for eyes
and frayed red string
for snarling lips.
it is true,
pins perforate the spot
where my fucking heart should be.
after all the people out there
who have had to bear witness
to my unpleasantries,
who have worn
my scarlet letter of suffering
and inconsiderate bullshit,
it is only right that this voodoo doll is
finally tearing
at the goddamn seams.

I've fallen madly in love
with an alternate universe
in which the mistakes
we've made are
holding hands, shambling
through the streets,
and laughing at the
triviality of it all

everyone
wants to be the muse
but what they often fail
to realize
is that they've
got to be
the heartache,
too

staying is sometimes a symptom
of fear but then again,
so is leaving.
and alcohol is the
only prescription for both.

either way,
we're all sick
and fucked.

it doesn't really matter which way
you play back our palindrome memories,
baby, we fell in love to Romeo and Juliet
by the Dire Straits, as we hibernated
in the gaps of our small town, and by the
time I realized I'd fallen desperately
out of love, and washed my hands of us,
we were already far too deep in
dire straits to claw our way out.

I can't pretend to
know what it means
when I crave a cigarette
as a non-smoker,
but maybe you can understand
that sometimes I want to
strip you of your layers,
and kick back with a scotch
while I admire you naked body
with no intentions of
fucking you.

the movies have ruined
us all.
the goddamn black
and white film
has turned our
feelings gray,
like you wouldn't
fucking believe.

maybe that's the problem.
we make heroes out of
drunks and sexed up
ideals and never thought
the requiem for the lonely
would catch up with us.

There's not a bookstore on
the planet I wouldn't stop in
just so I could play hide
and seek with all the dusty
souls blanketed in the prose.

the adults
you could never
tell them anything.

our voices were

simply white noise,

elevator music.

my mother once told me,
amongst the tantalizing chaos
and pain that stalked my blood,
"but you're far too beautiful
to be so sad,"
and I've spent every passing
moment since, trying,
for the life of me,
to figure out how the two
could ever possibly be divided.

we are far too broken
to be leaving pieces
of ourselves
in every undeserving person
that shows us
shallow affections

I can't say what's
moral and immoral,
but neither can you.

maybe the only moral acts
are admitting you can't tell
the difference when
faced with bloodshed,
and recognizing when you,
yourself, are the bloodshed

I'm running out of
goddamn metaphors, baby.
just please love me
enough to tell me
the truth about myself.

I melted into the couch
and listened to your
words breathe,
inflating me with
unjustified hope.
I felt you in my ribcage,
punching and struggling
against my
human metronome.
It was always you
and I'm just now
realizing that.

the fuckery of the
human condition is that
there no longer
is one.

now I know why people say
poetry is dead.
there's too many poets
with egos where their
souls should be,
instead they're rotting
into the pavement
outside my 4th story
window and even the
bums don't bother
to take the barely-used
mint-condition souls.

it occurred to me
that death only comes knocking
far too early
on the doors of the good,
the complex,
and the beautifully fucked up,
because he figures
if he's going to
feast on the world's soul,
then he might as well
make it fucking worth it.

how sad it was to discover that
there are people who no longer
read books,
but the true violence,
the goddamn epidemic of spirit,
lives inside those who do nothing
more than casually thumb through
one another and then ask
for the cliff notes.

little kids run through the schoolyard
at noon,
there's talk of guns, sex, and
robbing the corner store,
they toss profanity and death threats
to one another instead of a football.
there's neglect in the chests and
abuse behind their ribs.
with every utterance of "i don't care,"
i can see the light dim from their eyes
and possibilities erode from the dreams
they knew better than to have.
i chew on their words and think
they must be lost and in desperate need
of saving, until i realize that this,
this is the new found.

all we could do was
fuck and fight and
pretend the lightning
wasn't setting fire
to everything around us
that we once gave
a damn about

i'm glad i'm not a visual artist.
nobody should have to bear
witness to my grotesque
self-portrait,
the wilting skull
in the mirror smiling at my pain
and snapping my bones voluntarily
instead of dealing with the weight
of all the love i will always want
but never feel.

we only stay in love
with someone
for as long as we love
the person that we are
when we are with them.

according to that logic,
then I've never loved
anyone at all.

choke me lightly, aim for
the goddamn jugular if
you're going to do it
at all.
fuck the air out of
my lungs, fuck me senseless,
just don't fuck me up
(even more than I already am)

I am the death of poetry
and all things beautiful.

pour a glass of us
and raise your spirit,
I'll do everything I can
to drink in your disease.

people tend to bore me, they talk
too much and feel too little.
too often they're one-dimensional and
lacking substance.
the surface is an exact replica of
their blood and arteries,
even the cells have nothing interesting
to add.
baby, just know that there will
always be a difference between us
and them and I've got reason to
believe our love is a lucid dream
so wake me up when someone has
something new to say

we make beasts out of nothing
and expect our memories
not to scream.
follow the dying flowers,
hanging rag dolls
of sour petals, and find
us, in all our sun-starved
infamy, standing at the
beginning of everything.

she was a rolling stone,
emerald eyes, yellow hair,
and all. vagrant hands would
scribble of lost loves and
unburied remains.

what she never realized
was that the words she
was writing had become
more important that the one
she'd always told herself
she'd been writing
them for.

there was something in her
gait, she walked
like a secret that knew
it had been told,
but didn't mind one bit.

sometimes I think
that I'm impossible to love,
a fish caught, examined,
and thrown back to sea,
but no,
through my bourbon clarity
I came to realize,
everyone notices the death
behind my eyes,
the sinking weight of my despair,
and it's not that
they threw me back
for not being tender enough
or worth the fight to take home.
they unhooked me and
tossed me back in
because they only keep
the live ones,
you see.

the rain's shining,
the sun's falling
and you're absolutely
beautiful out.
      the sky's labored breathing
      leaves us flat lining on the
      country lawn and what
      a perfect day to die
      it is.

PART THREE:
ACID POETRY AND BATHTUB GIN PROSE

I'm fond of people
as long as the drinks
are bottomless,
the room is dim,

and the lights are
kaleidoscopes in my eyes.

if you don't turn your
oddities, your eccentricities,
into your life's work,
society will do its best
to make sure you're estranged
for them

the hardest thing in life
is to remain human
in a world in which
it's considered normal to
fall into a vacuum and
not even care to claw
yourself out

I think if people were
more honest with me,
I would hear a lot less of,
"it was nice to have
met you,"
and more of,
"it was quite strange
indeed"

an open beer to my right
and a brain that is trying
not to think in clichés.
that's what I'm equipped
with. maybe today I'll
punch out a poem on the old
typer that has the balls
to punch me back and then
watch me bleed out on
the floor.

my last words probably won't be
anything profound
and I'm perfectly okay with that.

I just hope that my labored whispers
reach ears that are listening.
do me a favor and spare me
the sentimental lies
at the celebration of my death.
if I wasn't thoughtful or sweet,
generous or understanding,
please don't tell everyone
that I imprinted the dirt of this world
with such pretty qualities.
I refuse to propagate untruths,
so instead,
tell them I constantly found my soul
at the bottom of a bottle,
not to mention my pathetic self-loathing.
tell them of my neuroses
and ability to alienate anyone
who has ever dared to love me.
my frayed edges will thank you.

so pour some tequila in my grave
to keep the worms and I company,
and toast to the fact
that I was a fucking asshole,
but god, did I mean well.

I was no match for
your cotton candy lips
and circus ring eyes.
the only thing I could
focus on anymore was
the thinning tightrope
between our half-hearted
acts and the hungry lions
waiting for us below.

I was never good at staying.
just ask the subjects of
most of my lustful poems.

once the sea breeze had settled
into the threads of our sheets
and salted the wounds
we had hidden from each other,
I was already halfway dressed
and searching for my stray sock.
I'm always down for a good fuck
but never was I more bitter
than when I cock-blocked
my own feeble attempts
to stay until
breakfast was served.

we had a lot to discuss
over bad coffee.

my continents are rattling,
oh dear, please tell me
I'm still soaked in madness.

after all these years,
you shouldn't be surprised that
I still chase every shot of you
with water and listen to
Fool In the Rain on repeat.

put your faith in my stubborn,
in my neuroses, and I'll teach
you to appreciate the sadness,
too.

I'm convinced that the
devil and god's top angel
got drunk on differences
and were weird enough
to each other
to one-night stand
my good for nothing soul.

freshly fucked and
ego bruised,
I light a smoke
and think that
love must be
just on the
other side of
crazy.

we looked like mad scientists
the way we made fire from scratch,

burning the entire headboard
off the fucking bed,

all the while wishing that
sophomore chemistry had been
a lot less chatter and
far more friction.

when I was 17,
I was bored more often
than not.
we all were.
every last one of our
vacant souls. it got to
the point in which
smoking a cigarette wasn't
just taking a break
from something. it became
the thing itself.
5 minutes
would pass and we'd stare
boredom in the face again,
no wiser than a pleading
bum with a misspelled sign.

I lit a cigarette as I read
what Camus had to say about
a senseless murder and I could
hear your familiar whispers
creeping in through my pores,
telling me that nothing
is senseless,
absolutely nothing.
I got so caught up in the twisted
images of you that I didn't
even notice my smoke had
burned out.

you never did get used to
my negligence and I
never learned to light
my own goddamn fire.

there's no perfect way to
say this so I'll just say it.
drinking you is in like
falling in love when
you're 8,
sharing a tree house
of secret clubs
and strawberry fields that
would stretch for days
when we needn't stretch
our grass-stained legs
at all.

if I could,
I'd tie helium
balloons to the
wrists and ankles
of everyone one of
your worries, lift
the horns right off
of those masked angels,
and invite you to
touch the sun
with me.
I'll be careful not
to let you burn.

we didn't end up fucking.
it somehow felt more
promiscuous that way.

that was the thing about acid.
you could never tell
if your poetry was falling
off the page or
if you were.

that face you make
when I nibble your hip bone,
make that again.

I'll admire every sliver
of you, if you'd let me.
I can't say that anyone
has ever made the mistake
of referring to me as
wholesome, but goddamnit,
this is the whole of me.

Love is like
a semicolon-
rare and hardly
used correctly;
It gets lost in
the mess of the
written word,
yet always sneaks
its way into
prose.

Why can't I
find someone
whose vertebrae
feel as inviting
as the spine
of an open book?

poets go to a different hell
than other humans.
I'll let you in on a secret.
it involves paralysis of the
voice box and hands,
and no one to fuck the
juices out of us.

I don't know about you,
but when I picture god,
I imagine him leaning against
the wall of a building,
maybe outside a smoky nightclub,
with a cigarette dangling lazily
from his lips, and dressed in
a slim-cut, navy suit- perhaps
his jacket swung over his shoulder
and his tie loosened like he
needs a scotch or three.
there are red-lipped women that
walk on by and smile flirtatiously.
he just nods knowingly.

bitch, you wouldn't believe
the things I've seen.

I think that if someone
called my poetry "pretty,"
then I'd be forced to
finish off their last
bottle of whiskey and
rape their toilet with my
acid poetry and
bathtub gin prose.

Are you fucking
unsettled yet?

No one ever
has it all
together and
that is the
most fucking
beautiful tragedy
about human
beings just
trying to be.

we're all actors
fumbling through
our lines
and tripping over
the props in the
worst fucking play
in the universe

I can't remember exactly when it was that
she went crazy but that's not nearly as
important as the why.
for years she reached out through the dense fog
and no one reached back,
no one dared to shatter the glass figurine of
her world, her borderline transparency
and cracks that went unnoticed.
when we met,
I handed over my world and she held it
carelessly between her fingers like the burning
cancer stick that it was.
what unadulterated strength she had,
I had seen nothing of the like.
goddamnit,
would you just stop and imagine her
on the rocks

soul mates are meant to reveal
the dirtiest layers of you,
your grass-stained ego and
singed fingerprints,
blistered heels and
calcified joints.

other's heartstrings tied
too tightly around
your throat and the seeping
vomit of regurgitated lies
that you've already choked on.

I'll apologize for the
crude imagery but your
soul mate won't.

there's nothing better to me
than learning your body,
becoming a pioneer of your terrain
and planting flags at each one
of your hot spots so I don't
ever forget
all the wonders I've seen
that weren't on the map
and the twists and turns that
would have tripped up mediocre
adventurers, too frightened
of the heights and too nervous for
the depths

I'm just a broken person
looking for other broken people
who may have gotten shards
of me stuck in their feet
and aren't too concerned
about pulling them out.

PART FOUR:
COAXING THE SCREAMING SUNSET

wish someone had
told me sooner that
the pursuit of happiness
meant the insatiable
appetite for whiskey
in my glass and a
naked body greeting mine.

I'da quit fighting the
good fight long ago.

let's plan our future
together in hell,
you do the
decorating
and I'll do
the drinking.

I'll never be certain
if she had gypsy
in her blood or
just too much wine
to allow anyone to
clip her wings.

the sun went down and
so did you,
each their own form
of art.
the sun, he took his time
painting the horizon
and tonguing the champagne
clouds,
but you, you wasted not
a damn second coaxing
the screaming sunset
right out of me

I just want to drink and sing
towards the sky and all
its wives.
I don't care if god doesn't
appreciate my strained falsetto,
because I know damn well
those tired angels don't play
their harps for nothing.

I look outside.
it's getting darker
earlier now and so is
my mind.
sometimes, I'm afraid
that I'm responsible for the
darkness, the sun's harbored
shame and the moon's lawless
gleam.
god, I think, while exhaling
my selfish mistakes,
if I even get it just a little
bit less wrong with you,
I'll know you're the angel I never
thought I'd want, the comfortable
lunacy I've settled into.

It was absolutely terrifying
to see the keys stick out of everyone's backs
like knives from a senseless homicide.
The wind-up toys marched in line
so as not to stray-
with their painted-on plastic smiles
and rosy cheeks,
you could almost be tricked
into believing the blood in their veins
was not the same slush
that's been regurgitated into toilets
far and wide.
If you ask me,
I'll take my island of misfit toys,
any day.

Look at the mess
I've made of us.

The poetic catastrophe
I'd always pined for.

I spent all night
giving birth to syllables
and their little harmonies.

Give me your raw soul
and I'll most certainly
tenderize it.

this poem is less of me
and more of you.
it's less about us and
more about you and I.
this poem is not cool,
it's not even fucking good.
it's just what happens when
there's an empty recliner
next to me and an even emptier
bottle of Jack.
this poem is not about
the love I lost but rather
the love I never found.

it started with a few
too many margaritas
(I'd recommend the
strawberry one if you're
ever in the neighborhood)
and ended with
piss in my bed.

there was loads of shit
in between but those
two are the most important.

the margaritas because
I hate tequila but
loved you and the latter
because you always needed
to be blackout to
to love me back.

the walls are going
to cave in sooner
or later,
it's just a matter of
whether you have
anything other than
a shallow soul
to break their fall.

sharing whiskey by
the fire,
what an impossibly grand time
we would have had
feeding off the
inexhaustible flames
of each other

I saw a hobo wearing my favorite
shirt today. I swear it was mine.
I knew by the frays on just one
sleeve and the confidence he had
as he strolled. I'd packed it up in a
bag of clothes and dropped it off
at good will the previous week.

When you had left our apartment
and scavenged every corner and
nook for what you could claim,
I couldn't stand the suggestive glare
that shirt gave me every time I
opened the 2nd drawer
from the top.

You always said I would be
buried in that goddamn shirt
and I just couldn't prove you right.

one of these nights
Jack Daniels is
going to get drunk
off 5 fingers of me
and wish he'd
never left that
damn bottle.

I've got a gun to my
head and it looks
a lot like society's
bullshit standards.

From the 1 % down to the poorest of poor,
we all share the same damn desires.
The rich can disguise them,
dressed up in pretty pearls
and cocktail parties,
philosophical conversations
and self-help books.

But let's tell it how it is-
we are all consumed by
the same fucking mundane things:
sex and food.

So let's ditch the dance floor,
find somewhere we can be alone
and when we're done round 5,
I'll wait patiently while
you preheat the oven.

I am skinned and ready
for roast,
my guard is down and
I'm dripping with sacrifice.
I can see your mouth
watering from here,
so what the fuck are you
waiting for?
I'm yours for the taking

we had our wine
and talked of cheating
death but you preferred
to keep me alive just
to watch me squirm.

you see,
you can love someone
and not like them at all.

maybe we've got it all wrong.
maybe love is meant to
save us from the very idea
that we need to be saved.

the writing process looks
a lot like expensive whiskey
I can't afford. it looks like
red-stained wine glasses and
half-smoked cigarettes that get
put out when an idea strikes.

it looks like fucking a story
out of a stranger and it feels like
falling in love with a car crash.

it's a lot of checking my bank
statement and progressively louder
sighs. but mostly it's just smiling
while I write your character
right in love with me.

i'll forever be the shack you never
thought you could leave,
the chipped paint and the stained carpets,
the fridge with nothing but beer in it.
the broken windows that allow the
brisk air to sneak in and the dirty dishes
flooding the sink.

i just hope that when you tell
people about my cobwebs,
that you tell then who
fucking made them.

it seems i've been on my way
to meet you all my life.
every vein i ever pumped
to excess with diluted passions
was a backed up highway
i should have gotten off
long ago. i'll be damned if the
headlights didn't look like
shimmering gold from afar,
but i guess Robert Frost was
on to something, after all,
and thank god i exited just in
time for me to crash into you

my eyes didn't quite know what to do
when they witnessed you playing in the
edge of the sea, pants rolled and
hair tousled,
daring the salted foam to kiss
your bare feet.
you were immaculate and I was stunned.
my pupils had to adjust just to take in
your light, and when they finally did,
I was rendered motionless,
paralyzed by all the things you can do
to me with your bonfire skin.
it's enough to make a believer out of
this eternally damned poet any day.

my love, I promise to always be
by your side,
absorbing the mayhem,
the very things that celebrate
your ever-fraying shambles.
twist your little insanities
around me in a smirking cyclone,

until all of your crazy
becomes my crazy too.

PART FIVE:
THERE MUST BE MAGNETS BURIED
DEEP WITHIN YOUR SKIN

3 A.M. HEARTBREAK MATERIAL

They were never of any
concern to me. The people
at the fancy nightclubs, the
ones getting bottle service
and straightening their ties.

I'd always preferred to indulge
in the deteriorating souls
at dive bars. the dirty, old
sacks of skin lighting their
6th cigarette after running out
of money to throw at the barkeep
and running out of expletives
to bark at lingering lovers.

I was high the second I laid
eyes on your suggestive lips.
I think my euphoric life had
something to do with the way
your smile crept across your face,
like the universe could wait.

forget a decanter-
the best way to
taste-test resurrected
grapes is off of
your tongue,

I breathed into you.

you shuddered in consent
like I knew you would.

if hell truly
does exist,
I'm willing to bet
satan took notes
when he watched me
watch you
walk away

where did you come from?
i don't know what to
make of you.
there must be magnets buried
deep within your skin.
i can't find mine but i know
that they're there,
polarized just for you,
fuck, what strong gravity ,
you're your own goddamn planet,
aren't you?
le petit prince fallen
from the stars and hungry
for human connection.

it was a night of cheap
red wine in an even cheaper
whorehouse.
sure, it didn't have prostitutes
but that didn't stop anyone
from being for sale.
everyone has their price
and mine was to be left alone
listening to The National
shake the walls and my skull,
so i sat back and drank
to the fact that all the wine
really was for me

it only cost a bottle
of pinot noir and
a joint passed between us
to understand that there
is a planet out there
falling out of orbit
while waiting for our
whimsical souls to arrive.

you are exquisite,
beauty preserved
in a glass case.
you are the answer
to the question,
"what moves you?"
the blinding hope
I never had,
the sun I willingly
stare into.

would you call me crazy
if I said,
you are the death
of death itself?

you were relentlessly there,
and it was beautiful
but for all
the wrong reasons.

oh how I'd kill
to have the punishment
I deserve,
to be a fly on the wall
in all the rooms
of our lives in which
I forgot to tell you
I love you

find a lover
that helps you to
get out of
your own way,
a lover that sees
a gorgeous infinity
inside of you
and holds a mirror up
for you to see it,
too.
get out of your
own way and
the world becomes
a whirling dervish
of opportunities.

It seems that
I've written myself
out of love with
anyone who has ever
had the nerve
to love me back.

I'm writing to say I'm sorry.
I'm sorry for putting you in parentheses,
for treating you like an afterthought,
postscript at the end of a letter.
but this, this is your letter,
too late, too pathetic,
not the one that should have
been about you.

you deserved a novel,
not the corner of a page turned down,
in case I ever wanted to pick up
where I had left off.
I should have taken the time
to read your footnotes,
to understanding the context of your smile,
of your tears, of the nightmares
that plagued you.

I hope that wherever you are,
you are doing well.
I'm sure that you are,
having been lifted of the heavy,
apathetic love
that once ailed me.

swallow a bottle,
breathe in the unusual,
I'd always preferred
my name in your mouth
than mine

I remember being bored
while you read the
novel of me. I recall
being surprised that you
could read upside down.
((fucking spoiler alert:
I die in the end.))

the language of the gods,
brutality and contempt,
dripping with fucks
(my mouth's still watering).

hollow me out until I'm
just a front and back cover,
one to hide my tits and one
to cover my ass,
and I'll perform for you the
greatest show of your life.

all of my life
I've filled rooms.
filled them with pride
and empty liquor bottles.
sometimes with lovers
I felt the need to punish.

the space was always
swelling with more of me
and my careless debris
and shriveling everyone else.

I can't wait to be
microscopic with you.

i wrote a suicide note the other day
without any intention of killing myself.
and i think you'll understand
what i mean when i say,
i needed a reminder that if i'm
still capable of dying then i must have
a fucking heartbeat somewhere
under here,
after all

I remember a time when you
really shook me,
you hurled your love-drenched
words at me and at one point
I used to pick them up off
the ground, woefully.
now I bet those words are
quiet as hell in their
comfortable, little coffins.

i just want to be left to read
my books, to drink, to fuck, smoke,
and write,
and between taking deep drags
of your love,
be recognized as the damaged goods
that i am, instead of
the monster under someone
else's bed.

the day i knew my angels had gotten
too high to remember you're not a love
that i deserve was the day in which
you curled up inside me with
more than enough leg room,
and you were pure, you were
fucking happy.
to this day i still buy my angels
the strongest bud to thank them
that you hadn't feared the very emptiness
of me,
the hollowed out soul i'd never known
i was until your unprecedented warmth
occupied it.

it occurred to me,
as I listened to you fall
gently to sleep,
never trust someone who claims
to love everyone.
that just means they don't
love anyone at all.
love holds no meaning to
people like them, and goddamnit,
do I love the fuck out
of you.

"the gods chose me
themselves, baby, you'll
see,
I can be good to you,"

"just be good to yourself,
it seems most people tend
to forget about that part"

living was
but a mere accident
and loving,
well, loving was the
flesh of our lives

a few minutes left in
Monday and you're sketching
skulls made out of charcoal.
as I watch your hand dance
across the page, I think
that I will consider myself
very lucky if I'm not
in love by Tuesday.

p.s.

you're everything I'm not,
and I can't imagine a greater
compliment than that.

AM HEARTBREAK MATERIAL

PART SIX:
CLIFF DIVING INTO JUGS OF WINE

you said ethiopian coffee
is your favorite as you
made us a midnight batch

you managed to hold the
tectonic plates of
my world together with
one hand and french press
we with the other.

to me,
peace and harmony
have always looked like
your naked, celestial body
sprawled across my
grateful sheets, while your
tongue tasted the stars
I was soon to borrow
from your palette.

you're captivating,
you're a beautiful desolation,
it's such a shame that we
have to ache the way that we do,
but it's deliciously tragic
that love is the one to blame.

sometimes i like to shrink and allow you
to fill up the room,
choke all the vacancies with your mist
and follow the scent of our bedroom adventures.
it's so goddamn pretty, the colors of you,
even the blues that normally keep
my depression company are kinder.
in these times i like to jump from typewriter
key to typewriter key,
a microscopic lover on a trampoline,
pregnant with silver dreams and words
i formed with my body.
and once you fill in all the empty space
that used to haunt my nights,
i sit back and smile.

the view from here couldn't be
more beautiful.

there's something quite
beautiful in knowing that
you're inconsequential yet
refusing to have anything less
than a tidal wave existence,
anyway

out of all the nights of
cliff diving into jugs of wine
and chasing the manic moonlight,
the memories i miss most are the
ones in which we flirted with
death just to taste its
sweetness and death
didn't know any better than to
flirt back

the people in bars
were always thumbing
through the cliff notes
of one another and
chewing on the nearest
soul just to spit it
back up,
and the worst part was
that they didn't take
delight in being mad,
with screws not only
coming loose but falling
out entirely, in pretty,
copper waterfalls,
and all they could do
about it was fuck
through the sadness and
get on the bottle again.

it's letting my foreplay
consist of rambling on nakedly
in bed at 2 a.m. about the gypsy
in For Whom the Bell Tolls
that lets me know
you must really fucking love me

the moon hangs loosely
tonight and
i can't lie,
there's times i wish
to join it

I showed up to the gates
of heaven, drunk and bruised.
you were hesitant, god,
to let me amongst your angels.
"But I've lived and loved
with all of my being,"
I pleaded between shots
of bourbon.
"you certainly have,"
you replied,
"it just wasn't the way
we like."

if anyone had told me
that paradise looked like
your toffee skin
and amber eyes,
maybe I would have
behaved a bit better
in my first life

the problem is,
all this time we've been
dying to be someone,
but we forgot to be
specific

if i had been eve,
in all her naked glory,
gleaning wisdom from
the serpent and letting her
tits bounce freely,
the apple would have most
certainly held promise of
promiscuous nights followed by
cold indifference with enough
self-loathing and fear
of abandonment to leave
everyone behind me
before they even got the chance
to desert me.

I heard a whisper that
you're a mysterious and
rusted skeleton key,
resold from street vendor to
unappreciative hands
and back again.
you've tried to wiggle
and jam into hundreds of locks
and you never quite fit.
forgive me for being rash,
but I plan to carve
its matching keyhole in
the door to my chest.
I beg you,
peel apart my ribcage
(delicately) and take what
has always been yours.

at one point I was so blind that
I only saw with my eyes.
now, as your soul smiles at me
from across the thick melodies of
Joe Purdy singing
"you're as far as I can see,"
I find comfort in knowing that
my vision's never been better.

all I ask is that you
remember the grays,
the ones that taunted
your sleep and teased
your dreams.
forget the black and whites,
the helter skelter
memories,
the apocalypse means nothing
without your crooked smile.

the lights were bright,
the street, inviting,
much like a stripper's
glistening ass cheeks,
and you were laughing
at the jokes I was
yet to make.

what a pretty
arrangement we had
but such an ugly execution.

you might call it destructive
the manner in which we smashed
each other's bones in a rum
& coke frenzy, but I just see
it as hollowing them out,
emptying the marrow, so that
we can be sure, when we decide
to fling ourselves off of the
Ben Franklin bridge, drunk
with calamity so beautiful,
that we will fly without
any fucking wings and
we will love without them too.

coffee black- it's 2 AM,
the night reveals her
promiscuous disposition,
and after months of courting
the moon in all his shapes,
she challenged him,
"go ahead and dazzle me."

I've dated too many purely
soft souls
who didn't have any fight in them,
whatsoever.
all I ever wanted was a lover
who wasn't afraid to punch back
whenever my monsters
came out to play.
now I have just that and
never have I been happier
to have a fat lip and black eye
when you lean in
to kiss me goodnight.

I've built goddamn monuments
to the mistakes we've made
and the bad blood between us.
even to the fucking age-old
coffee stain on the
living room carpet.

you had told me not to
choose beige,
you're too clumsy, you said.
and I, I was too in love to stay.

I'd built monuments to our
tangled whispers into the void
and I've since knocked them down.

I could feel myself
getting restless,
the tide tugged
at my roots.

maybe your touch
would feel familiar
again
once I leave my
footprints on
the moon.

perfume yourself
with spilled bourbon
and reincarnated memories
of me that you had
always prided yourself in
forgetting

stop referring to sex as
making love.
there's a deep romance in
fucking her dreams right out
of her head.
there's romance in shoving her
up against the wall and
stealing the air from her lungs
with an expert sleight of hand.
look her in the eyes and
hunt her down, silence her
fears with the tip of your
tongue, enough for her to
disengage and watch yourself
from above.
smack her ass, pull her hair,
tie her up and drink her
in, choke the very doubts
out of her

there's really only one
thing that I know for sure,
and that is that there are
divine parts in every one
of us and there are
tragically messy parts.
you can't expect to appreciated
the beauty until you share
a drink or 7 with the
disheveled piece that always
has a bar tab but never
actually pays.

my love,
I just want to comb through
the shipwreck of you,
your sunken, coral vessel.
I'll toss out the wood
chips, see what beauty
I can salvage,
and try not to choke on the
dust of lesser loves that
were forced to walk the
plank and swallow the dark
sea when they no longer
appreciated the treasure
that they had when
they had it.

I had been too much wine
and not enough bread,
too much overflowing sin
and not enough repentance,
a drunken angel
steering a capsized vessel.
bruised and demoralized,
I collided with the
earth's rancid soil.

now I am too much body
and not enough blood,
but you quite like this flesh
that I adorn
so we fall into your sheets,
you on your knees looking at me,
it's a prayer I know
I can learn to love.
as your tongue speaks below me,
I make the sign of the cross
out of habit,
and your sweaty altar bursts
into frenzied flames.
baby,
I bet you hadn't known,
but devils,
we can cry too.

smoke rings
aren't the
only O's
happening
tonight

this is how it ends, isn't it?
me drunkenly burying
an empty coffin in the backyard
just to convince myself
that you didn't leave
because you wanted to.

PART SEVEN:
3AM HEARTBREAK MATERIAL

look at us now.
nursing from bottles
our mothers didn't
give us and pretending
it isn't a gradual
suicide.

You don't need a knife
or a gun in order
to kill someone.

Just turn down the music,
look them in the eye,
and tell them that
you never loved them.

where do you go when we kiss goodnight?
tell me, is it to the times before
the fights,
the 10 round boxing matches in the
kitchen turned to ring?
it seemed so important at the time,
to be the one left standing on the cold,
tile floor,
bloodied and proud,
but alone in my celebration.
i'd check the time, always after 2 AM,
we'd punch the clock just to
bruise one another,
and retreat to our corners with images
of lost loves swirling in our
concussed skulls,
with nothing but future scars and empty
solitude to show for it

I don't believe anyone
would argue if I said
that you're 3 AM
heartbreak material.

i am full with drink
as the night is full and
the moon shines in
through the window like
it's been chasing you
all its life.
god, i hope, i beg,
it doesn't catch you,
i won't stand a fucking chance

when I said I wanted to be
with you forever,
I meant it,
it's just that the you
I had been referring to
hasn't shown face in months
and I've grown tired
of waiting

tie me up and nibble on my
collarbone, tease me til
the dusk succumbs to dawn,
and I'm a canvas of
murderous light.
fuck the dreams out of my
pretty little head,
make room for the bigger ones
I'd never thought to have.
I am yours
and I am more,
pleased to be misunderstood.

What a privilege
it was to be
irrevocably mad
and how magical
it was for you
to love me
when I was.

I couldn't find it in me to believe
you could love me and the mess
I made.
You'll forever be the balloon
I let go of in the middle of the street,
the hopes I still muse over
in between the darkest hours.
I'm still high off your helium and
how easily you lifted me.
You're the reason I don't look
both ways before headlights
and 3 AM slam into me.

it was only when I'd drenched
myself in jack honey and
hallucinogenic insomnia
that I recognized the eerie
symmetry between
desolation and
you

come to me in the dead
of night and
I'll show you all the
reasons the monsters
under my bed
are scared shitless
to reveal themselves

I was in love with you
until I wasn't and
that was that.
I don't think the ending
makes the middle any
less beautiful but
goddamnit,
I could have
chosen a more polite way
to ruin you.

I can hear your words float
through the fog from next to
my hospital bed. maybe I've always
been dead inside,
a coma patient nourished by tubes
and worried love,
and maybe you've always been
the distant voice begging for me
to wake up.
I should have listened, baby,
I should have fucking listened.

your empty vessels that
long to overflow
with the love of another,
know no superficial
discrimination as to what
satisfies them most.
there is no gender,
no skin, no weight,
and no hair.
just the alchemy of
the soul that finally
changes your heavy grief
into the transcendent beauty
it always knew it could be.

and when we fall into bed
together, two sweaty vessels
blanketed by humid potential,
we'll write thousands of stories
that no one will ever read
and that's quite alright, baby,
it's quite alright.

your heavy breathing reminds me
of a symphony and every string
instrument is in perfect tune
except for the goddamn harps;
my angels got so hot and bothered
they forgot their parts in the
sweaty refrain.

though there have been many
lovers who came after you
and managed to bring my
vagrant soul back into orbit,
back from my drifting lunacy,
I can't help but admit that
my blood still boils
at the thought of
your tilted world.

the moment I knew
I had fallen in love
was when I couldn't
distinguish between
being alone and
being with you.

you are more
myself
than I am.

some people have fucked
my quivering heart
until it has shattered
and I've turned those
whores into poetry.

the truth is,
I could never love another.
and I think you know that.

with one hand on your drink
and the other on tonight,
let's fall so desperately
into each other
that our guardian angels
get too drunk to stop us.

it's true,
i either chain-smoke or
don't smoke at all,
so i hope you understand
when i say i prefer to
either fuck you till dawn
or leave you tasting
the loneliness

it's true,
towards he end I felt latitudes
and longitudes away from you
even when there was nothing but
blue moon kisses between us.
I hadn't wanted to leave,
but somewhere along the drunken line
of our love,
I realized the map had never
been drawn to scale.
you showed me beautiful mountains
and I gave you nothing but rivers
to drown your eyes.

you couldn't have been
more perfect
and I couldn't have been
less ready.

rave on,
like the savage
tornado that you are

I'll surrender myself
to the spinning
and calamity if it
means destroying
everything with you.

it's true, the world
will never give me
another you. I have to
murder that notion nightly,
as the ice in my
neglected drink slowly melts
and drowns my trampled soul,
your ghost takes a sip
of my cheap whiskey and
I laugh, because loving you
never was easy.
still isn't.

drinking is the only true means
of time travel
that we poisoned vessels have.
but the bottle,
it doesn't have a number pad.
we can't decide
which memory we visit
once the ghosts of whiskey past,
tequila present,
and spiced rum future
take ahold of us.
it's fucking russian roulette
the size of a shot glass.

sing to me while I
play with the fire of
your skin, a cocktail
of beauty and violence,
an unfiltered arousal.
I swallow your embers,
the drugs my momma
always warned me about,
and spit them back out
the whites of my eyes.

I hope you like what
you see, baby,
the twirling nature
of your love.
throw some gasoline on
that fucker and we'll
watch from the rooftop
as this degenerate city
learns what romance
really is.

cocaine kisses,
draw blood from
my lower lip
and let it drip
into your nightcap,
make sure my blood
is your blood
by the time the
sun comes up.

it was a 4 AM kind of night.
i made you a drink as you walked
in the door and reminded me
of my place in the world.
you have always had this contagious way
of warming the room like
new year's eve breath.
you looked at me and sucked down
your white rum.
the only things that stood between us
were a blunt and the promise of inertia.
trust me when i say
i'd never known a movement so enchanting.

you climbed on top of me
and somewhere,
trumpets roared.

232

people talk of heaven
as if it's a distant
place,
and I can't help but
wonder who it is
they fall asleep next
to every night.

We need to stop labeling those who celebrate
what they are good at as cocky or arrogant.
It's teaching society to hide behind shrouds
of diseased self-esteem and insecurities.
I know what I excel at and I know what needs
a fuck ton of work.
For every negative of mine,
a better picture is trying to scratch its way out
from under my skin to reveal itself.

It's true, I'm messy and sometimes vain,
inconsistent and selfish, tragically unsound.
I drink too much, this I know.
I can be impulsive and I fuck up omelets sometimes.
But in the same breath,
I'm intelligent and thoughtful,
I can laugh at myself and can occasionally be profound.
I am deeply caring and sensitive,
a true romantic,
as much as I have tried in the past
to pretend that I'm not.

It's scary to think what we could accomplish
if we dare to empower one another.
Can you image a world
so pure, so warm?

PART EiGHT:
PROSE PROSE PROSE

It's strange to see him again...

It's strange to see him again. Cameron, that is. No matter how many times I have tried to stop myself from the decadence of sleeping with him, I have always felt myself going back to him. Sometimes I managed to trick myself into thinking that I never had feelings for him, but once my cover was blown, my feelings would come back full force and with reckless abandon. Either way I always found myself drunkenly stumbling over to his house at all hours of the night.

"It's been a while," I say, almost off-handedly.

"Yeah, it has," he agrees.

It's all he really can say. He feels the need to mention who's getting to know his bed now. Good thing I sat on the edge. I nod my head robotically, "Yeah, that's cool."

I need a cigarette so that I have something to do with my hands, but when I pat my pockets, I find that I don't have a pack with me.

The same sexual tension that I always felt around him isn't there, and if it is, I can't feel it. And just because you can feel it, doesn't mean it's there anyway. I don't have the compulsion to become reacquainted with the ghosts of these sheets, and then to wake up in the morning wishing we'd never met, like a hangover that wasn't worth the drink. And that's a good thing, because I don't think I could stand another ride on that goddamn carousel without getting sick.

Fuck it, that's a god honest lie.

I'd sacrifice motion sickness for another night with him any day. Who am I kidding? But, all I know is that I don't want him to check my closet because I'm afraid of how many skeletons he will find- a pile of bones for a suit of skin that I don't feel comfortable in

Forgiveness

We waltzed hand in hand into the nearest pub to escape the late winter's bite. I wondered off-handedly if anyone had ever bitten back. It was a cosy nest of drinks and floating eyes, eyes with no prior engagements whatsoever, no dates to be had, no plans to be avoided. We found two vacant seats at the bar. Kyle rubbed my hands for warmth and I pulled away. His grasp felt more like that of a straitjacket than a lover's. War was inside everyone and it burned to stare at their suns. Out of all the empty fish bowls, there was one man I saw that I recognized. I'd seen him years before. At the time, he'd been bright-eyed and dripping with a confident clarity about him. His hands had been calloused by honest work and a 7 o'clock drink, but this time he had the eyes of 360 hangovers within a year's time and the palms of a man who had held a heart he'd known was about to shatter, yet set it on the ground to be trampled all the same. I knew the feeling well. I could see the cracks in his skin and the dullness in his eyes. He had been given the chance to hurt and he'd taken it.

This man, he didn't recognize me. I was sitting a few too many feet from him to innocently start conversation and Kyle was eyeing me wearily. I inched my seat towards his shadow and ordered a whiskey on the rocks. The bartender danced around the bar, a marionette controlled by my craving. The puppet to my right, Kyle, ordered a craft brew that probably made him feel distinguished. I hope it made him feel that way anyway. There was a cold indifference in his eyes but I knew it wasn't his own. It didn't belong to him and it never would. The frozen battlefield was the sight of me reflected in his green mirrors. I turned away and offered the jaded man a smoke. I thought maybe he'd offer me his tale of despair back but he didn't. He accepted the cigarette and I was momentarily pleased. Within my next two staggered breaths he snapped the cancer stick in two. I then understood that he ruined the perfectly good smoke the way he'd ruined a perfectly good woman's spirit. It was his silent confession of the crime his rough and experienced hands had committed. The gradual murder.

For the goddamn sake of love, I nodded to let him know he'd been forgiven. I raised my glass and absolved him of all his sins. I don't need to tell you that it was beautiful for you to know that it was.

I'm not sure if he understood but I never saw him again and I didn't want to.

To My First Love...

To my first love, although it didn't last, in my mind we are still in the midst of it. We may not be together but I am like Jupiter nonetheless, revolving around the sun that was our love, and jealous of the one who wears a ring next to me. I think of those summer days when we first met and it was a competition to see who could stumble over their words more. Our eyes stayed glued to the stars that had already died and little did we know, we were staring at the light our love shed as well, right before exploding into blackness.

We discussed our future dog, a topic which I had refused to budge on. We would have a red, female dachshund (wiener dog) named Ruby, and her eyes were to be green. How funny it is that I bought a chocolate, male dachshund, Romeo, named after our favorite song, "Romeo and Juliet" by The Dire Straits? In a way, I'd damned myself to think of you every time he cried in the dead of night or wanted to cuddle on my shoulder, the same way in which you always found refuge next to me in my bed that was never big enough for the both of us.

Maybe I wasn't everything that you wanted me to be, but I was all that you needed me to be. You could never walk me to my doorstep and kiss me goodnight but a drawn out kiss in the car down the street was enough for us. We were enough. It's been years since and when I look back, I don't see pain but I see the most fun two people could have ever had together. Your jeep retired with the gentle exhaustion of our love and I wouldn't have had it any other way. The image of us speeding down the highway with the top down is forever seared on my mind and our careless laughter echoes off of my four, blank walls when I have no music to drown it out.

I guess what I'm trying to say is, thank you for a love so pure and true- a period of my life in which the snow was always white, and no one trekked dirty boots on it. Now, every time I look out the window, it's pollution and muddy footprints that I see.

I'll Remember You

There was a girl. Her bedroom always resembled the center of a tornado in order to match the catastrophe occurring inside of her head. The first time I saw her, I was half in love with her by the time she made her way over to me- you know, that wretched waltz we do in the name of romance. I was fully in love with her when she mistook me for someone else. She stayed and chatted anyway, which she didn't have to do and then just as quickly as she sprang into my life, she was whisked away by a gentleman most displeased. I imagine this is because he saw the gleam in my eye and came to realize that her blue-green eyes were now my captor. I laugh now as I pour a generous amount of whiskey in my glass. Anytime I would refer to her eyes as "blue-green," she would shrug her shoulders and then laugh this manically endearing laugh. This was because she knew that I was in love and that I'd lie to the end of the world just to see a smile break across her face. Her eyes were a pure blue, the kind that hasn't been tainted with.

She dips her toes into the water's edge, as the ocean kisses the shore and then retreats with his hands in the air: a fashionable date rape.

"Come feel, the water is warm."

"Just a minute, babe...let me finish what I'm writing."

"Tragedy will always be around, but I might not be," she says mockingly, putting one hand on her hip.

I drink the ink from my pen and try not to feel like a cliché. I put my cigarette out on a seashell and laugh out loud at the irony of my poison joining nature. We're all damned in the end anyway, but I seem to be in a hurry.

She tilts her head back and takes a big swig of her beer and her freckles look electric in the mid-afternoon sun. She leans in half-heartedly to kiss me and I turn my head.

"No," I resist.

"You're beautiful, alluring, endearing, radiant, inevitable, even. Your touch is static, your eyes, hypnotizing, but I think we both know we are at the end of the road."

That knowing smile creeps across her face and I suddenly, irrationally, hate her, like I've never hated anyone before. I want to tell her this but I'm paralyzed. The sand under my feet is hard and I forget that I'm at the beach, not in my own kitchen, catapulting china wear across the room just to make a point. Breaking expensive things feels good when your relationship is nonexistent, cheap, at best. The devil's vapor escapes her lungs and climbs the unforgiving horizon. I breathe her in, neglecting all the consequences, because falling in love with a stranger is such an easy thing to do. The owner of her heart comes jogging towards us (her), unintentionally heroic. His jaw is set, purposely flexed, and his eyes are locked in, begging for a release. His smile is goofy and relaxed, as if I am an empty threat to him. He swoops in and kisses her like no one has ever kissed someone before, and I can see her body tense up in rejection, but no one feels it but me. I'm forced to admire her from afar while he is given the world. She and I are like diamonds poorly shaped- cut and molded with our flaws as evident as gold. He picks her up, weightless in his arms, shows her what a conventional, safe, suburban romance looks like, and she hardly even glances back at me.

Floods

There was rainfall the past few days. I'm sure of it. I didn't witness the rain but I could hear it from the isolation room. I don't belong here, I think, as I return to my normal routine on the ward.

There's the man that won't stop whispering to himself about how he and his alter ego should kill the staff. For some reason the workers don't seem phased by this, though. Then there's the old woman with prunes for hands. I swear she's possessed by the Devil. I saw her slam her head into the toilet once. On purpose. I wasn't supposed to be in the bathroom at the same time as her but I really had to pee and couldn't hold it. That's what happens when you're pregnant. The baby sits on your bladder. Whenever I used to wash my hands next to a pregnant woman in the bathroom, I'd smile at them like we were in a secret urination club. I am lucky enough to have three babies sitting on my bladder. I imagine they must fight a lot in there, taking turns doing belly flops onto it and whatnot. They make it awfully hard to focus on anything, including my hourly prayers and sacrifices, with all their kicking and tumbling.

When Toilet Woman sees the sun she starts to scream. It's this awful, inhuman screeching sound. It interrupts my afternoon stroll. The only time that I find peace. God likes to talk to me on these walks. He leaves bouquets of flowers in secret places just for me. Sometimes he smiles at me from carvings in tree stumps. God is chivalrous, quite unlike the modern-day men that I've met. He and I, we once got into a horrible fight, as all couples in love do, and I apologized to the staff and crazies repeatedly for the storm that damaged the roof but no one seemed to accept my apology. The possessed woman spit on me, which made me happy. The staff kept talking to me in quiet and comforting voices.

Oh, I forgot about the young, Spanish man that thinks he's dead and that everyone around him is a ghost. He doesn't bother me a whole lot except when he walks right into me. I'm transparent, in his eyes. I love the look on his face after that happens, though. He furrows his brow and shakes his head violently before speed-walking away from me.

After I wait in line to take my pills, a man I've never seen before walks towards me, with grace and confidence. I know that this is Him. He's come to me in human form to help me raise our children. The scruffy face, the tousled, sandy hair.

"Don't speak. I know a place we can go," I whisper against his cheek.

He nods and takes my hand. We sneak off into the woods and my screams of pleasure sound eerily like Satan's in the sun.

My Favorite Nightcap

The flashes from drunken cameras are extra bright tonight. Everyone's capturing blurry moments and I'm drinking at the bar alone. In the brief moments between photographic lightning when the darkness disguises everyone's faces, I think how my bed is like a dark room. It's the only place Robyn and I have ever been developed. I never wanted to be her midnight musings or her 2 A.M. toss and turns, but I found myself saying things I never meant anyway. I never wanted to be her 3 A.M. "I wonder if she's still awake" or her 4 o'clock anxious plans. If only I could flip back through the script and write the truth in, edit it with red pen. Maybe then I could be okay.

I order a glass of whiskey, neat, and smile at the pretty bartender. As I say thank you, I bite my lip and chew on my words. *Who am I kidding?* She'd be another wasted night, anyway. I'm like Adam in that painting on the ceiling of the Sistine Chapel. People have tried but no one has ever quite reached me.

I stumble and run into people on my way to the bathroom. I turn on the cold water and lower my face towards the sink. I splash the water onto my face and smack my cheeks but it's no use. There's no waking up from this coma. I glance into the mirror and my eyes look dead. Except for that, I do make a goddamn good impression of myself. Nonetheless, I feel stranded in front of my own face. The women who come out of the stalls stare at me weirdly as they join me at the sinks to wash their hands and evaluate their appearances. I wish I could help them to feel beautiful, but tonight I don't have the strength. Instead, I take a cab home and stare at the cracks in the ceiling that look more like the faults in the earth's surface. It feels as if for my entire life I've been driving through a tunnel at night. I don't know *when* the hell I'm gonna reach the end.

The one thing I'm sure of is that you don't need a knife or a gun in order to kill someone. Just stumble home from the bar, lips wet with whiskey, look them in the eye, and tell them that you never loved them.

Coffee Stains

I pour myself a cup of coffee and drink it black. Cream in the morning, naked at night. It helps me to sleep. This is very confusing to people to understand. I sit up in bed and read a few chapters Nine Stories by Salinger. I decide that Seymour did what was right for him and then I slide down the bed to set the book on my nightstand. I don't fold the page down. I know that I'm on page 13. I lie awake and muse over my dreadfully dull day. Well, I didn't die today, good for me. But then again, I might as well have if that's the most noteworthy thing I did all day. My TV is droning and the white noise lulls me to sleep.

The morning arrives like a 16 year old boy losing his virginity. Coffee with cream. There are no eggs for me to fry so I get in my junker and drive a few miles down the road to a seedy grocery store. There are plenty of eggs to choose from. It's all very overwhelming. I think I should start getting my groceries delivered again. I choose a random carton and go to check out. I try my best to avoid small talk with the cashier. Surely small talk is a cruel joke told by Satan. As I go to get into my car, a man in a hoodie and 5 day beard walks up to me casually. Oh no, more small talk. He puts the barrel of his gun against my ribs and tells me to hand him my keys. I stare at him and he asks if I'm a retard. I don't think so, I say. I like his hoodie and almost ask him where he bought it but quickly realize that would be absurd considering the circumstances. Then fucking move, he says through gritted teeth. Dull human teeth. I'd rather like to keep my car, I say. Shoot me if you want, I add as an afterthought. His eyes grow big and I examine his pupils. The irises swell but the pupils remain slits. He glands around to see if anyone's watching but of course no one is. If no one's fucking or fighting, humans have no desire to pay attention to anyone but themselves.

Natural beasts.

I don't want to have to kill you, man, just hand over the keys. I think I'll keep them, I say. I'm rather indifferent to the pistol jabbing me except for the mild discomfort. I think of my eggs and wonder if they've cracked. No, of course not, Rob. They're sitting like kings on the passenger seat. I don't know what the hell is wrong with you but you need some serious help, man, he says as he turns to run away.

He turns around once to look at me and I feel more beast than man.

I check on the eggs. Perfect condition. I drive home, get back into my robe, and fry up some eggs. There's a knock at the door. I open it to find Karen gazing into me. It's quite disconcerting but I don't tell her that. She strolls on past me and helps herself to some bourbon. Five fingers for me, I say.

She comes into the living room, hands me my glass and sits down. She looks transparent, too. I tell Karen of my morning adventure and then check on my eggs again. She's aghast.

Weren't you scared he'd kill you?
I'm not sure. I think I was more afraid that he wouldn't kill me.
You're so depressing sometimes, Robert.
I like to think it means that I'm still thinking.
Do you love me?
I'm not sure. I've grown quite used to you.
That's not reassuring.
It would be difficult to become unused to you. I may not know if I'm in love but you're a habit of mine.
I'm crazy enough to love you, you know.
I never asked or you to be.
But everyone eventually wakes up from their reverie and I'll be there waiting at the edges of hell when you do.

What do you think that man is doing right now?
The bearded man? Probably killing time outside a liquor store. Murdering each person that walks by, in his mind. In his head he's the world's greatest assassin. He'll never pull the trigger, though.
Neither will you.

We kill the bottle of whiskey and I think how maybe that man needed his little victory. I took that from him. Karen starts lifting her dress up and I lift my eyes. I rise and she notice. I pick her up and carry her to my bedroom. I bite the bottom of her dress and command the very fibers of her. I nibble on her hip bone and her body squirms below me. Her collarbone feels neglected so I leave my mark.

We soon start to make it like it's a goddamn new idea and she falls asleep shortly after. I glance out the window at the bridge I don't care to know the name of. More people seem to have been jumping off of it lately than crossing it. Pennies. Pennies dropped into fountains and the empty hands that belong to even emptier humans. Change is a mirage painted by the world.

Another knock at the door. The old man from the 15th floor. It doesn't matter much to me whether he's here or not. He asks for a beer with a hand already in my fridge. As long as he doesn't touch my cheese. I don't want to try my luck at the grocery store again. He opens the beer on the edge of my table and I shout for him to grab me one. We guzzle down our drinks, probably for different reasons. All monsters look the same form the outside looking in.

The old man lights a cigarette and picks up the unread newspaper on my coffee table. His eyes dance briefly across the page the flicker up at me. You've got to read this story, he says. Give me the summary, I say.

This fucker broke into a family's house and demanded a goddamn puppy. A puppy, Rob. The family told him they didn't own a dog so he ran off with a copy of The Fountainhead.

That's the greatest story I've ever heard. It's nice to know there's at least one thief who has his priorities straight.

You're a twisted man.

I'm not sure I mind.

Do you believe that really happened?

I don't know that what I think is necessarily important. Some mornings I wake believing in everything and by lunch I believe in nothing.

After a few more beers it seems that old man has grown bored of me. Tell the lady hi and bye for me, he says. I say I will even though I'll forget. Forgetting is the easiest way to exist, the best evolutionary adaptation. That's why the Neanderthals didn't survive then. Those big memories didn't stand a chance.

I light a cigarette and start to read Nine Stories again. I wish that I could find a bananafish at some point in my life. It would mean a lot to me.

Karen wakes up and pours herself a wine. She's ass naked and her body swims through the air.

Darling, I had the most horrible dream. A man tried to steal your car and you told him to shoot you.

You don't say.

It was terrifying how indifferent you seemed to be to dying.

I can imagine, baby. What a goddamn mess that would be.

But you're alive and drunk. Just how I like you.

I go into the bathroom to check the mirror. Normally there's smudges where my eyes should be and sunken in cheek bones. Tonight I smile at myself. The frightening, possessed grin of a clown that's died a thousand times over. It seems perhaps I've been taken off life-support. The feeding tubes no longer litter my sorry excuse for a soul and my shadows dance for the first time since I've met them. I didn't die today.

Good for me.

Underwater Mountains Publishing.
Elias Joseph Mennealy & Ryan Christopher Lutfalah.
A Private Company.

Made in the USA
Lexington, KY
11 March 2015